TOP 10
BASKETBALL
SLAM DUNKERS

Peter C. Bjarkman

SPORTS
TOP 10

ENSLOW PUBLISHERS, INC.

44 Fadem Rd.   P.O. Box 38

Box 699   Aldershot

Springfield, N.J. 07081   Hants GU12 6BP

U.S.A.   U.K.

Library of Congress Cataloging-in-Publication Data

Bjarkman, Peter C.
  Top 10 basketball slam dunkers / Peter C. Bjarkman.
      p. cm. – (Sports Top 10)
  Includes index.
  ISBN 0-89490-608-9
  1. Basketball players–United States–Biography–Juvenile
literature. [1. Basketball players.] I. Title. II. Title: Top ten
basketball slam dunkers. III. Series.
GV884.A1B53 1995
796.323'092'2–dc20
  [B]   94-45889
                                                       CIP
                                                        AC

Printed in the United States of America

10 9 8 7 6 5 4 3 2 1

Photo Credits: Frank P. McGrath, pp. 6, 9, 10, 13, 14, 17, 19, 21, 22, 25, 30, 33, 34, 37,
38, 41, 43, 45; Naismith Basketball Hall of Fame, pp. 26, 29.

Cover Photo: Frank P. McGrath

Interior Design: Richard Stalzer

CONTENTS

Introduction

THEY ARE PERHAPS THE GREATEST acrobatic athletes in the entire history of professional and amateur sports. They fly through the air with a power and grace that can simply never be matched by baseball players or muscular football players. They are also some of America's biggest stars in an age when television images and music videos rule the nation's airwaves. These are the men who perform in the National Basketball Association (NBA) and their game is now the acknowledged king of the entire sports world.

Basketball is today a game of larger-than-life heroes and nonstop action that is perfectly in tune with America during the 1990s. Here is our new national sport that has replaced baseball and football as the game of choice for millions of young and old fans alike. Nothing is more responsible for the popularity of the new winter sport than the high-flying, rim-jarring dunks of airborne superstars like Michael Jordan, Shawn Kemp, Charles Barkley, and Clyde "The Glide" Drexler.

Basketball was once a game largely earthbound in its style of play. Its heroes were once skillful ball handlers and expert passers like Bob Cousy of the 1950s Boston Celtics or tall, agile shot-blockers like seven-foot Wilt Chamberlain and long-armed Bill Russell. Chamberlain and Russell could easily dunk basketballs but seldom used this tactic. By the mid-1960s, however, a new excitement popularized a faster-paced style of basketball, an excitement provided mainly by sharpshooters like Oscar "The Big O" Robertson, "Mr. Inside" Elgin Baylor, and "Mr. Outside" Jerry West. Yet basketball never fully captured the public imagination until the arrival of Julius "Dr. J" Erving and Connie "The Hawk" Hawkins in the early 1970s. Hawkins and Dr. J suddenly took the indoor game above the rim with a new style of slam-dunking acrobatics.

Basketball's most popular dunker and its biggest hero is Chicago Bulls superstar Michael Jordan. Charles Barkley of the Phoenix Suns brings thunder and explosiveness to his powerful slams. Tiny five-foot-seven-inch Spud Webb of the Sacramento Kings defies gravity and demonstrates that even small men can elevate their game far above the steel rim. The electrifying Darrell Griffith in Utah earned his title as "Doctor Dunkenstein" with an endless variety of miraculous moves as he flew over defenders and soared above the hoop.

The ten NBA superheroes profiled here are among the most spectacular slam dunkers of pro-basketball history.

CAREER STATISTICS

Player	Career	Average	Points	Games	FG%	FT%	Rebs	FGM	FTM
CHARLES BARKLEY	'84–	23.3	17,530	751	.562	.734	8,734	6,259	4,683
DARRYL DAWKINS	'75–'89	12.0	8,733	726	.572	.685	4,432	3,477	1,777
CLYDE DREXLER	'83–	20.7	17,136	826	.480	.786	5,105	6,584	3,591
JULIUS (DR. J) ERVING	'71–'87	24.2	30,026	1,243	.506	.777	10,525	11,818	6,256
DARRELL GRIFFITH	'80–'91	16.2	12,391	765	.463	.707	2,519	5,237	1,387
CONNIE HAWKINS	'67–'76	18.7	11,528	616	.479	.779	5,450	4,144	3,235
MICHAEL JORDAN	'84–'93, '95–	32.3	21,541	667	.516	.846	4,219	8,079	5,096
SHAWN KEMP	'89–	14.5	5,552	383	.508	.716	3,374	2,075	1,397
SCOTTIE PIPPEN	'87–	16.9	9,302	551	.491	.683	3,765	3,778	1,571
SPUD WEBB	'85–	10.1	6,638	657	.456	.833	1,465	2,410	1,593

CHARLES BARKLEY

The game's most ferocious power forward, Charles Barkley slams home a monster dunk for his former team the Sixers.

DURING THE 1993 NBA PLAYOFF FINALS, Charles Barkley made certain there was almost as much excitement off the court as there was during the dramatic games themselves. Barkley drew attention, just as he always has, with his colorful and sometimes shocking public statements. "Sir Charles" was at his best with the media during the spotlight of championship play. "There will never be another player like me again," Barkley told the press. "I'm the ninth wonder of the world."[1]

Barkley's Phoenix team would not win the NBA championship in 1993 when they squared off with Michael Jordan and the powerful defending-champion Chicago Bulls. The Suns would battle courageously for six games—including an exciting triple-overtime contest at Chicago Stadium—before a last-second shot would give Chicago its third straight NBA title. But when Phoenix lost their first challenge for the title in seventeen years, it was not because of any lack of effort on the part of their star player, Charles Barkley. Barkley kept the Phoenix team roaring back each time it looked like "Air Jordan" might make a runaway of the championship series. He matched Jordan with 42 points in game two and then led his team in both scoring and rebounding in four of the championship contests. The game's most ferocious power forward was again flashing the same brilliance he had displayed all year, a brilliance that had already brought him the NBA 1993 Most Valuable Player award and recognition as *The Sporting News* player of the year as well. Sir Charles was doing exactly what had been expected when Phoenix management had traded away three veteran players to acquire him from Philadelphia a year earlier.

While Barkley kept the opposition on their toes and the fans entertained through the championship round, he kept the press satisfied as well with his endless stream of postgame witticisms and boasts.

Barkley has always been controversial both on and off the court. While playing for the 76ers in Philadelphia, he often publicly criticized the owner and his teammates for not wanting to win badly enough. Charles has always put winning and hustling at the very top of his personal goals. But the outspoken athlete has also had other more important and serious messages for his legions of admirers. Most recently he has made a television commercial in which he tells young fans that he should not be their hero or idol just because he can dribble and shoot and rebound. Youngsters should idolize their parents and teachers, Barkley warns, not glamorous professional ballplayers.

On the court, however, Sir Charles is one of basketball's most ferocious rebounders—although a relatively short front court man at six feet six inches—and has averaged more than 800 rebounds for each of his 10 seasons. The most memorable aspect of Barkley's play is his fierceness under the basket and around the rim. The typical Barkley maneuver is to grab a defensive rebound, lumber the full length of the court like a runaway truck, then slam home a huge dunk that intimidates his foes and electrifies the crowd. Indeed the most terrifying sight in basketball—perhaps in all of sports—has to be the image of this huge and agile 250-pound athlete roaring down the floor and toward the enemy basket, determined to fly through, if not over, any defender daring to block his path. With his large but finely toned body, Barkley has been the most physical basketball player of the past decade.

CHARLES BARKLEY

BORN: February 20, 1963, Leeds, Alabama.

COLLEGE: Auburn University.

CAREER: 1984–

NBA: Philadelphia Sixers, Phoenix Suns.

POSITION: Forward.

HEIGHT: 6′ 6″

Charles Barkley remains the "Round Mound of Rebound" with his new team, the Phoenix Suns.

DARRYL DAWKINS

Darryl Dawkins, the first high-school player ever drafted to the NBA in the first round, sweeps the boards for the Sixers.

DARRYL DAWKINS

DARRYL DAWKINS WILL ALWAYS LIVE on in basketball legend as the slammer who once provided one of the most destructive dunk shots in all of basketball history. But the muscular, fun-loving Dawkins was also a most special pro-basketball pioneer in still another important sense. For Dawkins had surprisingly come directly from the high-school courts of Orlando, Florida, straight into the NBA. Although hundreds of colleges descended on Orlando's Maynard Evans High School with scholarship offers for the six-foot-eleven-inch schoolboy star, Dawkins boldly decided that his game was already too advanced to belong anywhere except with the physical and talented pros. The Philadelphia 76ers agreed by making young Dawkins the first high-school player ever drafted in the first round of the NBA draft.

Virginia high-schooler Moses Malone had also signed on directly with the pros in the rival American Basketball Association only one season earlier. A lesser known player named Bill Willoughby would also graduate directly from scholastic play in New Jersey to the Atlanta Hawks the same winter as Dawkins. Malone, of course, would soon become one of basketball's all-time greats, but Willoughby would not. Dawkins, for his own part, proved quickly enough that he did indeed belong in the NBA. One night at the beginning of his fifth pro season, the giant center suddenly and surprisingly earned a special brand of basketball immortality.

The first to smash a backboard or rip down a rim was not Shaquille O'Neal or David Robinson or any of today's high-flying NBA stars. It was a powerful forward of the 1960s named Gus Johnson. The NBA was a lesser-known league in those days, and such events hardly made the sports pages or appeared on television news. More than a decade after Gus Johnson, however, the game of pro basketball had already become a premier spectator sport. It was in November 1979 that backboard bending got its first headline attention. The legendary player who first stamped his signature on the game by shattering a glass backboard during a league game was the towering center of the Philadelphia 76ers, Darryl Dawkins.

It all happened less than a minute into the third quarter of a game in Kansas City, and it was a moment that has now become one of basketball's greatest memories. It happened so fast that those in the audience who might have blinked for a second missed the entire spectacle. The huge and powerful Darryl Dawkins swept at the hoop from the right side of the court and slammed home another of his famed bone-jarring dunks that had so often entertained fans around the league. But this time the result was quite different. The backboard simply exploded under the force of the awesome attack, and glass splinters rained down on Dawkins and the playing floor around him. A stunned defender, Bill Robinzine of the Kansas City Kings, along with courtside spectators, scurried to escape the sudden shower of splintered glass.

Dawkins was always as quick with witty boasts as he was with his power moves to the hoop. On this occasion, he would explain to reporters that an uncontrollable force of "Chocolate Thunder" had simply escaped from his body. Whatever he chose to call the display of power, however, the sport had never seen anything quite like it.

It also took the poetic Dawkins a week to come up with a fitting description of his memorable slam, eventually dubbing it a "Chocolate-Thunder-Flying, Robinzine-Crying, Teeth-Shaking, Glass-Breaking, Rump-Roasting, Bun-Toasting, Wham-Bam, Glass-Breaker-I-Am Jam."[1]

DARRYL DAWKINS

BORN: January 11, 1957, Orlando, Florida.

COLLEGE: None.

CAREER: 1975–1989.

NBA: Philadelphia 76ers, New Jersey Nets, Utah Jazz, Detroit Pistons.

POSITION: Center.

HEIGHT: 6′ 11″

"Chocolate Thunder" rules the rim as Darryl Dawkins stuffs one for the New Jersey Nets.

CLYDE DREXLER

Demonstrating his impressive skills, Clyde Drexler makes a power move against the Indiana Pacers.

CLYDE DREXLER

PRO BASKETBALL FANS WERE TRULY excited about the 1992 NBA Finals matchup between the Chicago Bulls and Portland Trail Blazers. The league's two most powerful teams would lock horns in the best-of-seven series to crown a new NBA champion. For the first time in several seasons—since Larry Bird had last battled Magic Johnson—two of the NBA's most spectacular players would be facing off head-to-head as well.

Michael Jordan would carry the banner for the Bulls in their attempt to repeat as NBA world champions. The Portland club was returning to only its third final round ever. But this time Portland was equipped with an almost equally spectacular athlete to lead its championship charge. Clyde Drexler would have the chance to show that he was every bit the center stage act that Air Jordan had long been.

While in college at the University of Houston, Drexler was such a spectacular dunker that he and his teammates were nicknamed "Phi Slamma Jamma" for their soaring and slamming style of play. Male college students often join social clubs known as fraternities that feature three Greek letters for their names. The sporting press was suggesting that the exclusive social club to which Drexler and his teammates belonged in Houston was the flashy basketball squad that twice fought its way to the Final Four of the NCAA championship tournament while Drexler was the team's high-scoring star. It was during these college days that Clyde Drexler first displayed a rare leaping ability and hang-time skill that allowed him to seemingly soar above the rim and float effortlessly above his opponents. It was this rare skill that had earned him the colorful nickname of "Clyde the Glide" long before Drexler had arrived as a new star on the NBA horizon.

Now in late-season 1992, Clyde the Glide was ready to soar to new championship heights. Drexler had indeed waited a long time for this chance to showcase his talents before the widest-possible basketball audience. For years he had been a headline player in one of the league's smallest markets. Many nights he had been truly spectacular in leading Portland to three straight seasons of 57 or more victories. He had climbed to the top of most Portland all-time team record lists, ranking first in club history in scoring, games played, minutes played, field goals made and attempted, free throws made and attempted, and steals. But a stellar performance against Jordan would now perhaps provide the needed final stamp of approval on his often-overlooked career. A team championship would even further enhance his reputation as one of basketball's brightest stars.

Portland would not win the championship against the powerful Chicago Bulls. But Drexler would have several chances to test his talent on Jordan's own stage. He would first lead his team to a dramatic overtime victory in game two at Chicago Stadium. Then several nights later he would pace an attack that would allow the Trail Blazers to remain alive with a homecourt win in game four as well.

In the end, Drexler was gracious in his defeat by the great Michael Jordan: "I don't compete against Michael and I don't play for recognition. What I can do for Portland is all that matters."[1] In the 1992 NBA Finals, however, Drexler had done all three, despite his modest denials. He had competed head-to-head with Jordan and held his own, averaging 25 points per contest for the series and exploding for 32 points in game three. He had shown the entire NBA world what fans in Portland already knew, that he was one of the league's most skilled and glamorous players.

CLYDE DREXLER

BORN: June 22, 1962, New Orleans, Louisiana.

COLLEGE: University of Houston.

CAREER: 1983–

NBA: Portland Trail Blazers, Houston Rockets.

POSITION: Guard.

HEIGHT: 6′ 7″

"Clyde the Glide" Drexler hangs above the rim.

JULIUS ERVING

THE YEAR WAS 1976, and the scene was McNichols Arena, home of the Denver Nuggets. This was not today's NBA but instead its short-lived rival, the American Basketball Association (ABA). The star of the moment was one of basketball's most familiar faces. A young Julius Erving wore the uniform of the ABA New York Nets. The sell-out crowd was stone quiet as Erving paced off seven steps from the foul line, then turned toward the hoop and sprung into flight. Leaving the floor just inside the free-throw stripe, the graceful Erving soared toward the hoop and descended with a rim-bending slam. The first and only ABA slam dunk championship matchup had come to an end.

It is a celebrated fact of sports history that Julius Erving is the inventor of slam dunking as a basketball art form. The man they call "Doctor J" is, after all, the original high flyer— the incomparable player who, more than any other, pioneered the free-flying and gravity-defying game of modern professional basketball. Before Dr. J came along, the hardwood game was still largely earthbound. But when Erving first arrived as an unknown college star from the University of Massachusetts, he introduced a revolutionary kind of offense that instantly turned heads and opened eyes everywhere. By the time he had become an established star with the Philadelphia Sixers of the NBA, all other high flyers were being compared only to him.

Many veteran basketball watchers have been awestruck by Julius Erving's explosive style of play. "There have been some better people off the court," observed then Los Angeles Lakers coach Pat Riley, "like a few mothers and perhaps the

JULIUS ERVING

Dr. J (Julius Erving), the inventor of slam dunking, hangs in mid-flight on his way to the basket.

Pope. But on the court there is only one Dr. J the basketball player!"[1] Erving's own coach with the New York Nets, Kevin Loughery, was quick to note that "Doc was the first guy to fly, and he did things with a basketball that nobody else has ever done."[2] Dr. J, it seems, had just as strong a hold on the pro-basketball game of the 1970s as Michael Jordan would have two decades later.

The young Erving, who first exploded on the pro scene in the early 1970s, was most especially inspiring. The most amazing thing about Dr. J was that he always saved his finest and most thrilling performances for the biggest games. In the 1976 ABA championships he single-handedly led an average New York Nets team to the league title over a much more talented Denver ball club.[3] His physical features, including his huge over-sized hands, allowed him to grasp a basketball as if it were a softball. His long-stemmed, slender build—as much as his spectacular mid-air moves—truly set him apart from all the other great stars of the game.

Julius Erving first electrified crowds in the less popular American Basketball Association. For several years, he seemed to carry the entire struggling league on his broad shoulders. He invented a new style called "hang time," and it immediately became the most popular attraction in all of basketball. It even altered the very nature of the sport. Fans crowded into ABA arenas to see Dr. J lead his team to victories. They were also amazed as he made his spectacular moves around defenders and toward the enemy hoop. Here was the first great pro basketballer who was not measured by the points he scored, or by victories he engineered, or even by stats he posted in any other area of the game, such as rebounds or assists or shooting percentages. Erving was judged only by the artistic performances he provided night after night as basketball's greatest one-man aerial show.

JULIUS ERVING

BORN: February 22, 1950, Roosevelt, New York.

COLLEGE: University of Massachusetts.

CAREER: 1971–1987.

ABA: Virginia Squires, New York Nets.

NBA: Philadelphia Sixers.

POSITION: Guard.

HEIGHT: 6′ 7″

Julius Erving's outstretched arm is ready for the stuff.

DARRELL GRIFFITH

Darrell Griffith, the original "Dr. Dunkenstein," solos during the 1985 NBA Slam Dunk Contest in Market Square Arena, Indianapolis.

DARRELL GRIFFITH

MANY MAY CLAIM THE TITLE of basketball's most colorful slam dunker. Julius Erving invented the hang-time approach to playing above the rim. Michael Jordan captured the imagination of an entire generation of hoop fans with his soaring moves to the bucket. Shaquille O'Neal and Charles Barkley can lay claim to the most bone-jarring and rim-rattling power moves the game has ever known. But when it comes to legendary nicknames based on high-flying feats, none can surpass the man they once called simply "Doctor Dunkenstein"—the crown prince of dunk.

Darrell Griffith earned his reputation as a high-flying basket stuffer several years before he became a professional. His reputation for breathtaking aerial moves had spread nationwide even before he was selected as second overall choice in the 1980 NBA draft by the Utah Jazz. The six-foot-four-inch guard was already unstoppable by his second college season. Three times he was a college All-American, and in his senior season, the sportswriters had chosen him College Player of the Year for 1980. It was a well-deserved selection for the stylish guard who displayed a variety of entertaining dunking moves every time he took to the floor for the University of Louisville Cardinals. This showman was a winner as well as a crowd pleaser. As a senior, he would take Louisville all the way to a national championship victory over UCLA during the season-ending NCAA tournament. This is college basketball's greatest showcase event.

Griffith was at his spectacular best in that 1980 NCAA Final Four battle between Louisville, UCLA, Iowa, and Purdue. Rarely before or since has a single player so dominated college basketball's final weekend shoot-out. First, he single-handedly dominated Iowa in the semifinals to the tune of 34 points, 6 assists, 3 crucial steals, and even 2 blocked shots from his outside guard post. In a less-than-well-played championship game with UCLA, it was Griffith's dramatic jumper that broke a 54–54 deadlock and provided the needed winning basket. Doctor Dunkenstein was again the title game's leading point-maker with 23 points and the Final Four Most Valuable Player as well. It was the fitting conclusion to a spectacular four-year collegiate career for the player who had become a legend even before he had graduated from Male High School in Louisville. He had been so spectacular as a high schooler that many believed Griffith would bypass college play altogether in order to sign on directly with the city's American Basketball Association franchise. Darrell Griffith had long dreamed of an NCAA title, however, and in the spring of 1980, that dream had reached fulfillment.

Soon Darrell Griffith was proving he could outjump and outmaneuver opponents in the talent-filled NBA arenas as well. Griffith entertained the fans with his popular high-wire act of soaring above the rim and slamming home surefire thundering dunks. He surprised NBA skeptics everywhere with a brilliant first season that earned him Rookie of the Year honors. He had hammered home better than 20 points per contest as an untested rookie, played the second most minutes on his Utah team, and owned the team's second-best totals in points, scoring average, field goals, and steals.

The spunky Griffith had a few other tricks up his sleeve as well. Unlike many other dunkers who focus their game on inside play close to the bucket, the versatile Griffith was soon shooting aerial bombs from long range as well. In 1984 he would lead all NBA scorers in 3-point shooting accuracy. This is a rare feat indeed for a man whose reputation was first made by soaring over the rim.

DARRELL GRIFFITH

BORN: June 16, 1958, Louisville, Kentucky.

COLLEGE: University of Louisville.

CAREER: 1980–1991.

NBA: Utah Jazz.

POSITION: Guard.

HEIGHT: 6′ 4″

Darrell Griffith of the Utah Jazz elevates his game above the rim.

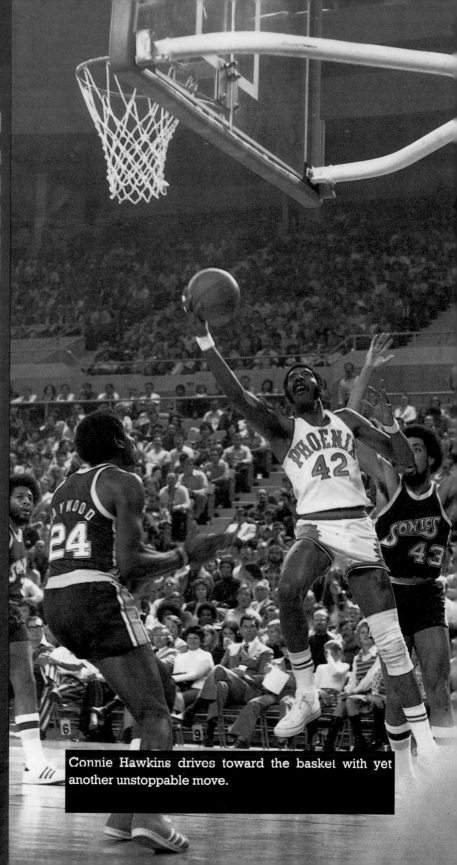

CONNIE HAWKINS

Connie Hawkins drives toward the basket with yet another unstoppable move.

CONNIE HAWKINS

IT WAS PERHAPS THE MOST EXCITING head-to-head matchup between two potential new stars in the history of the National Basketball Association. In the late fall of 1969, the Milwaukee Bucks, one of the league's newest expansion teams, were about to host another expansion club, the Phoenix Suns. But the real attraction for fans this night promised to be the anticipated battle between Milwaukee's seven-foot-two-inch rookie center Lew Alcindor and the Suns' outstanding six-foot-eight-inch forward Connie Hawkins. Alcindor (later known as Kareem Abdul-Jabbar) had recently led UCLA to three straight national championships. Hawkins was considered a legendary scorer from the playgrounds of Brooklyn who had already starred in the rival American Basketball Association. Now he was bringing his game into the NBA.

For several years, the NBA Board of Governors had blocked the former playground star from their league. He had once been implicated in a college point-fixing scandal, despite the fact that later investigations proved Hawkins innocent of any type of wrongdoing. Now the ban had finally been dropped.

Promoters knew that the real question on the minds of fans for this dream matchup would be whether Hawkins could employ his many unique offensive moves to penetrate the defensive wall of the huge and talented Alcindor. The marquee outside the Milwaukee arena that night hadn't even mentioned which teams were playing. It simply read "Connie Hawkins vs. Lew Alcindor."

The game started somewhat slowly as Hawkins and Alcindor both appeared to be only feeling their way. They appeared wary of each other and of their new surroundings in an NBA arena. But suddenly Hawkins slid across the floor like a giant panther about to strike at his target. The Suns' forward shot from the right corner of the court, gathered up a pass, and soared over the startled Alcindor—and the rim as well—for an unstoppable dunk. The young Milwaukee center barely recovered in time to slap the ball weakly aside. But a goaltending violation was instantly called against Alcindor who had arrived a second too late to stop Hawkins.

Hawkins would soar past Alcindor on several occasions that memorable night. The late-arriving rookie would score 19 points, make 50 percent of his shots, and also grab 7 rebounds against his taller opponent. Connie Hawkins had passed his first test in an NBA arena and had proven what all had long suspected. Hawkins was indeed everything that those who had seen him in the weaker ABA league had promised he would be. He had the spectacular moves and all the physical ability needed to dominate his opponents— whoever they might be—just as he had always done since his earliest days as a Brooklyn playground legend. At twenty-eight years of age, Connie Hawkins's best years were already behind him, and he would never again be quite the dominant scorer he had been just a few seasons earlier in the lesser American Basketball League and the rival American Basketball Association. But few could now doubt that even an aging Hawkins was one of the sport's most spectacular and entertaining stars.

As great as Connie Hawkins might prove to be, however, the expectations surrounding his game would perhaps always reach beyond the possibilities of his performances. Those who saw him in Milwaukee that night in 1969 knew that Connie Hawkins needed no such comparisons. For here was a star who would soon write his own unrivalled basketball legend.

CONNIE HAWKINS

BORN: July 17, 1942, Brooklyn, New York.

COLLEGE: None.

CAREER: 1967–1976.

ABA: Pittsburgh Pipers, Minnesota Pipers.

NBA: Phoenix Suns, Los Angeles Lakers, Atlanta Hawks.

POSITION: Forward.

HEIGHT: 6′ 8″

Connie Hawkins stuffs one against the Atlanta Hawks.

MICHAEL JORDAN

Michael Jordan unleashes his classic airborne style at the 1985 NBA Slam Dunk Contest in Indianapolis.

MICHAEL JORDAN

THE NBA CHAMPIONSHIP FINALS of 1991, pitting the Los Angeles Lakers and Magic Johnson against the surprising Chicago Bulls, was the greatest challenge of Michael Jordan's sensational basketball career. Jordan had already led the NBA in scoring for five of his first seven seasons. He had been the league's most sensational star and had averaged better than 30 points per game for five straight seasons. But Jordan was still haunted by the notion that he was not a true basketball champion. He had often read comments in the press that he and his team could never seem to win the big game when championship play started up each May and June.

The critics had found plenty of reasons to argue that Jordan—for all his flair and all his prolific scoring—was not yet a true championship player. Although Jordan had soared to unmatched individual achievements, his Bulls team had remained always earthbound. With Michael hurt throughout much of the 1985–1986 season, the team had limped home more than 20 games under .500 and failed against Boston in the first round of the postseason playoffs. The embarrassing first-round exit from postseason competition would continue only one more season. The Bulls climbed into the conference finals in both 1989 and 1990, but they still could not overcome the powerful Detroit Pistons. The Pistons had no Michael Jordan but featured a much more balanced and potent all-around attack. Jordan was accused by fans and press alike of not making those around him into better performers. He was even called a selfish player.

Now Jordan and his teammates had actually reached the NBA Finals after several seasons of play-off disappointment.

Yet failure appeared to face them squarely once again. Despite 61 victories by the Bulls in regular-season play, the Lakers appeared to be in command of the title series. They had already captured the first contest of this championship round. Chicago and Jordan appeared to have the opening game comfortably in hand on their own home court until the final moments of play. Jordan, as usual, led all scorers with 36 points, yet Jordan missed a crucial jump shot in the waning seconds that would have put the game on ice. Then Jordan's former University of North Carolina teammate Sam Perkins stole the game away for the visiting Lakers with a dramatic three-point bucket.

Game two found the evenly matched teams again deadlocked in the final quarter. Something truly dramatic was needed, and Michael Jordan had always been basketball's most dramatic player. Jordan soon took command as he grabbed a loose ball and sped toward the basket. Air Jordan soared over the hoop and slammed home a thunderous dunk. Moments later the Bulls had buried the Lakers, 107–88, and were finally on their way to a sweep of the final four games. Jordan had used his ultimate weapon—a monumental dunk—to seal the most important victory of his career.

From his earliest season in 1984, Jordan had been an unstoppable scorer who averaged more points per game (32.3) than any player in pro-basketball history. He was also a master of shot blocking and a fierce defender. But it was Jordan's airborne charges to the basket—his tongue hanging out and his legs and arms spread like a giant eagle—that would so inspire the nation's fans. Most spectacular of all was the naturalness of Michael Jordan's leaping and soaring game. "I don't plan all that stuff," Jordan has often remarked, "it just somehow happens naturally."[1]

MICHAEL JORDAN

BORN: February 17, 1963, Brooklyn, New York.

COLLEGE: University of North Carolina.

CAREER: 1984–1993, 1995–

NBA: Chicago Bulls.

POSITION: Guard.

HEIGHT: 6′ 6″

"Air Jordan" electrifies a Market Square Arena crowd in Indianapolis with a power slam dunk.

SHAWN KEMP

Shawn Kemp appears to be bound for the upper atmosphere as he stuffs the ball through the net.

SHAWN KEMP

WHEN SHAWN KEMP FIRST STEPPED onto the arena floor of the huge Seattle Coliseum in November 1989, he was in awe of all that surrounded him. An untried basketball newcomer was about to debut in the fabulous National Basketball Association. His opponents this opening night would not be the powerful Los Angeles Lakers or legendary Boston Celtics. They were only the lowly Minnesota Timberwolves, a first-year expansion team that was as new to the league as he was. But Shawn Kemp still had every reason to feel very much out of place. He was a rookie of the rarest sort, one whose previous playing time had not been earned in big-time college basketball arenas but only on the unglamorous high school courts of Elkhart, Indiana. Shawn Kemp had never played a single minute of college basketball. Now as an untried rookie, he would jump straight from facing smaller and less-talented high schoolers to battling the greatest basketball players in the entire world.

Kemp was in rare company indeed. Only four previous players had ever stepped straight from high school into the NBA. A forgotten pioneer named Joe Graboski had first made such a leap with the old Chicago Stags in 1948. This was in the days when pro basketball was still a small-time barnstorming sport that enjoyed few fans and even less media attention. Darryl Dawkins, Jim Willoughby, and Moses Malone had all made the same jump in the mid-1970s. But only Malone and Dawkins would become stars.

Shawn Kemp was therefore facing a challenge that few athletes before him had dared to tackle. It did not take the youngster from Indiana long, however, to demonstrate to everyone who followed basketball that he was more than ready for his most special basketball destiny. Only halfway through his unusual rookie year, Kemp became an immediate celebrity. He took his spot as the youngest entry ever to compete during the Gatorade™ NBA Slam Dunk contest showcasing the league's All-Star Weekend. The six-foot-ten-inch sensation was not only a most unusual rookie, but a most unusual rookie with considerable flair.

In each of the next four seasons, Shawn Kemp's stature grew by leaps and bounds in the star-studded world of NBA basketball. He led his Seattle team in rebounds three times, and in blocked shots every season. With an 18-point scoring average in 1994, he became the club's leading scorer as well. Kemp only truly arrived in the eyes of most fans, however, with yet another slam dunk contest appearance, this one in the Charlotte Coliseum during his second pro season. On this single afternoon, the millions of fans of the NBA discovered what Seattle boosters already knew. Shawn Kemp was one of the newest and brightest of true NBA superstars. It was the dunking game that had indisputably clinched Kemp's new-found star status.

During his first slam-dunk competition in Miami, Kemp had been a mere untried rookie at only twenty years of age. He had appeared awed by his more experienced rivals, like two-time winner Dominique Wilkins—Atlanta's "Human Highlight Film"—and defending champ Kenny Walker of the New York Knicks. Despite a few impressive first round jams, Kemp never made it into the finals that first season in Miami. Yet it was a more confident Shawn Kemp who showed up in Charlotte a mere year later. This time he would barely lose in a final round head-to-head battle with Boston's rookie Dee Brown. But, Seattle's Kemp had already proven he was next in line among the game's slammers and jammers.

SHAWN KEMP

BORN: November 26, 1969, Elkhart, Indiana.

COLLEGE: None.

CAREER: 1989–

NBA: Seattle SuperSonics.

POSITION: Forward.

HEIGHT: 6′ 10″

Looking to break away, Shawn Kemp is surrounded by the opposition in a rare earthbound moment.

SCOTTIE PIPPEN

A team player, Scottie Pippen reaches for the rim and another score for the Chicago Bulls.

SCOTTIE PIPPEN

IT IS NOT EASY TO PLAY on the same team with basketball's greatest living legend. Scottie Pippen found that out soon after he joined the Chicago Bulls in 1987 as an All-American from tiny Central Arkansas College. It was immediately obvious to all who watched the Bulls that Pippen was destined to be a great star in his own right. He was a player of almost unmatched offensive skills, one who could shoot the ball from anywhere on the court. He owned an impressive array of offensive moves that were certain to make him a deadly scorer as well as a guaranteed crowd-pleaser. Foremost in Pippen's large offensive arsenal was a devastating dunk shot that was already the envy of opponents and fans everywhere he performed. Yet few appreciated what a rare talent Pippen truly was. Everyone who came to see the Bulls play, or watched them perform on television, seemed capable of seeing only one Bulls uniform in action. Everyone came to see number 23, Michael Jordan, and largely ignored the star's other highly talented teammates.

Of course Pippen was already used to displaying his special brand of basketball magic far from the limelight. He had performed his collegiate heroics far from the glare of the television cameras and the notice of the sporting press that focuses on the big-school play of the major conference universities. The Arkansas native had averaged 26.3 points per game during his senior season—one of the highest marks in the nation—and yet few outside of a handful of knowledgeable NBA scouts had even noticed.

But if Scottie Pippen was a truly great and a largely unappreciated player, he was also a remarkable team player.

In an era when athletes often seem selfish and complain loudly if they do not immediately reap the glories they think they deserve, Pippen was quite different. He played hard night in and night out and contributed to Chicago's great team in every way he could. His scoring average steadily improved from his rookie 10.0 mark to 21.6 by his fourth season, and his playing time more than doubled over the same stretch. He evolved quickly into one of the league's best young defenders. His slick play at both guard and forward positions was a perfect complement to the all-world performances of his more famous teammate, Jordan. Pippen all the while patiently waited to share the media limelight.

When that turn came, Pippen was more than ready for it. As the 1993–94 NBA season opened, Michael Jordan was suddenly absent from his familiar spot in the Bulls' lineup. Jordan had retired early to pursue the dream of a pro-baseball career. Now Pippen was finally left to lead the Bulls.

When the league's best players gathered for the 1994 All-Star Game in Minneapolis, Minnesota, Scottie Pippen was ready to make a statement about his new role as the Chicago Bulls inspirational leader. When he arrived on the floor of the Minneapolis Target Center, Pippen could hardly be missed for even a fleeting moment. As action unfolded in the showcase game, Pippen was in the spotlight.

Scottie Pippen had patiently waited for his moment of glory, and now he controlled the All-Star Game action and claimed his spot at the top of the league's superstars. As a one-man show, he scored 29 points as he shot 9 for 15 and also grabbed 11 rebounds. Pippen fittingly canned a difficult base-line jumper with only minutes remaining in the contest to secure a victory for his East All-Star squad. It was now Scottie Pippen who was the NBA All-Star Game Most Valuable Player.

SCOTTIE PIPPEN

BORN: September 25, 1965, Hamburg, Arkansas.

COLLEGE: Central Arkansas College.

CAREER: 1987–

NBA: Chicago Bulls.

POSITION: Forward-Guard.

HEIGHT: 6′ 7″

Scottie Pippen is in an airborne battle for the ball.

SPUD WEBB

HIS NICKNAME IS A SHORTENED version of "Sputnick" and refers to the first Russian space capsule launched into the heavens in the late 1950s. The rare name was actually given to him as a child and it has nothing at all to do with his present-day orbiting above the iron hoops of the National Basketball Association.[1] But now, as he stood poised for his first run and leap of the 1986 NBA All-Star Weekend Slam Dunk Contest, his nickname seemed so perfectly appropriate. He was, after all, a tiny space flyer able to magically orbit above all those larger giants who towered inches above him when his feet were planted firmly on the basketball floor.

Fans and sportswriters alike nonetheless had to scratch their heads in disbelief when the five-foot-seven-inch Webb first took the floor for basketball's most spectacular annual dunking exhibition. It is held each year during the gala NBA All-Star Weekend. Defending champion Dominique Wilkins, Webb's Atlanta Hawks teammate, was one of a handful of rivals, all of whom stood nearly a foot or more taller than the pint-sized flyer. The tiny Webb was up against some of the pro game's greatest leapers—Milwaukee's Paul Pressey, Portland's Jerome Kersey, and Indiana's Terence Stansberry.

But Spud Webb had a surprise in mind for his heavily favored competition. He was performing before his hometown crowd in the Dallas Reunion Arena. He beamed with the same confidence that had already propelled him over every possible obstacle on his way to an unlikely NBA career. If his height had not kept him out of the NBA in the first place, it was hardly about to hold him back now. Webb had only one response to questions from reporters who laughed

SPUD WEBB

Spud Webb flies through the air with the greatest of ease to score another 2 points for the Atlanta Hawks.

off his presence among super leapers like Kersey, Wilkins, and Stansberry. "I know I can win this thing," Webb calmly proclaimed.[2]

Dominique Wilkins appeared to be the one destined for the repeat title of champion dunker, however. Michael Jordan—a loser in the finals to Wilkins a year earlier—was injured and would not be competing this year, a fact that seemed to leave the field wide open for the spectacular Wilkins. Dominique—known as "The Human Highlight Film" for his thunderous slams and jams—rose to the challenge by scoring a near perfect 99 points out of a possible 100 during the final round. Wilkins appeared safe from any serious challenge. Wilkins' own brother, Gerald Wilkins of the New York Knicks, also wowed the crowd and judges when he became the very first dunker in contest history to soar over an inanimate object—the younger Wilkins leaped above a chair placed several feet in front of the basket to score a perfect 50 points in the preliminary round. But none of these fireworks were quite enough. Three straight times Webb amazed both fans and judges with his twisting slams and his own perfect scores of ten.

Webb would soon be conquering other seemingly insurmountable obstacles in the years following his unlikely victory in Dallas. He would also prove beyond a doubt that he could play day-in and day-out in the rugged NBA. Soon he would team with Dominique Wilkins to lead the Atlanta Hawks to four straight league playoff appearances. Several seasons later, he would be a regular double-figure point scorer in the backcourt of the Sacramento Kings.

It is safe to say that in a game populated largely by giants and near-giants, there has never been a more unexpected skywalker than the tiny aerialist who owns basketball's most perfect nickname. Spud Webb has been proving for almost a full decade that the gift of flight is not a big man's gift alone.

SPUD WEBB

BORN: July 13, 1963, Dallas, Texas.

COLLEGE: Midland College, North Carolina State University.

CAREER: 1985–

NBA: Atlanta Hawks, Sacramento Kings.

POSITION: Guard.

HEIGHT: 5′ 7″

Spud Webb almost seems to get lost in the sea of opponents as he leaps up for another seemingly impossible shot.

NOTES BY CHAPTER

Charles Barkley

1. Fran Blinebury, "NBA's Best: Profiles of Pro Basketball's Top Players" *Street & Smith's Pro Basketball Annual*, 1993–94 (New York: Conde Nast Publications, 1993), p. 18.

Darryl Dawkins

1. William Jemas, Jr., and William M. Gray, eds., *NBA Jam Sessions: A Photo Salute to the NBA Dunk* (New York: NBA Publishing, 1993), p. 47.

Clyde Drexler

1. Jack Clary, *The NBA: Today's Stars, Tomorrow's Legends* (Rocky Hill, Conn.: Great Pond Publishing, 1993), p. 25.

Julius Erving

1. Alexander Wolff, *100 Years of Hoops* (New York: Oxmoor House, 1991), p. 126.

2. Greg Garber, *Basketball Legends* (New York: Friedman/Fairfax, 1993), p. 32.

3. Nathan Aaseng, *Basketball's High Flyers* (Minneapolis, Minn.: Lerner, 1980), pp. 11–17.

Darrell Griffith

No notes.

Connie Hawkins

No Notes.

Michael Jordan

1. Jack Clary, *The NBA: Today's Stars, Tomorrow's Legends* (Rocky Hill, Conn.: Great Pond Publishing, 1993), p. 52.

Shawn Kemp

No notes.

Scottie Pippen

No notes.

Spud Webb

1. Spud Webb, with Reid Slaughter, *Flying High* (New York: Harper and Row, 1988), p. 11.

2. William Jemas, Jr., and William M. Gray, eds., *NBA Jam Sessions: A Photo Salute to the NBA Dunk* (New York: NBA Publishing, 1993), p. 78.

INDEX